**Books are to be returned on or before
the last date below.**

LIBREX —

My Jewish Community

Kate Taylor and Matthew

Photography by Chris Fairclough

W

FRANKLIN WATTS
LONDON•SYDNEY

©2005 Franklin Watts

First published in 2005 by
Franklin Watts
96 Leonard Street
London
EC2A 4XD

Franklin Watts Australia
45-51 Huntley Street
Alexandria
NSW 2015

ISBN: 0 7496 5882 7

A CIP catalogue record for this book
is available from the British Library

Printed in Malaysia
Planning and production by Discovery Books Limited
Editor: Laura Durman
Designer: Ian Winton

The author, packager and publisher would like to thank the following people for their
participation in this book:
    Matthew's family
    Matthew's friends, Dillon and Gil
    Glasgow Maccabi
    The Jewish Telegraph Group of Newspapers
    Rabbi M. Rubin
    Giffnock and Newlands Synagogue
    Ruth Levey
    Calderwood Lodge
    Hello Deli

Photo acknowledgements: Corbis p19 bottom.

Contents

All About Me

My name is Matthew and I'm seven years old. I am *Jewish*.

I have lived in a place called Newton Mearns all my life. It's just outside Glasgow city centre. Quite a lot of other Jewish people live here too.

I live in a house with my 3-year-old sister, Maya, my mum, Hazel, and dad, Mark.

► **Me and Maya outside our house.**

Me and Maya have our own bedrooms. My favourite room in the house is the lounge. The sofas are really comfy and I can lie on them and watch TV.

▼ **When my cousins come round, we all sit on the sofa.**

My Family

My whole family lives in Scotland except for my Uncle Richard. I like having relatives nearby!

I get on with Maya most of the time, and she makes me laugh a lot. I'm glad I've got a little sister.

All my grandparents live just around the corner. They always pop in to our house to say hi or come over for lunch or dinner.

◀ My grandparents.

▶ **Me with my grandpa Michael.**

My aunt and uncle live nearby too, and my cousins Sam and Dayna come over to play a lot.

My Uncle Richard lives in London but he's moving to Boston in America soon. I hope we can go and visit him in the summer.

◀ **Me with Sam.**

Where I Live

I like where I live. It's nice and quiet and my neighbours are really friendly.

The road I live in is a dead end so there isn't much traffic. I play in the road with my sister and cousins, and sometimes our neighbours too. We usually ride our bikes and scooters or play football.

▶ Maya on her scooter.

There's a big park called Rouken Glen about five minutes away from my house. It has slides, swings, a roundabout and a huge climbing frame. Before, I could only get halfway up it, but I can climb to the top now.

My Community

The Jewish community in Glasgow has its own youth club and newspaper.

On Sundays I play football at Maccabi, the Jewish youth club. It's in a place called Giffnock, which is five minutes away from my house.

There are lots of different things to do at the club. They have a summer scheme for 5-12 year olds and organize trips. Last year we went to a safari park just outside Glasgow.

▶ **Some of my friends in the Maccabi football team.**

There's a newspaper in Glasgow called the *Jewish Telegraph*. It comes out every Friday and my parents always buy it. You can read about lots of things that are going on in the city. My football team was in it last week.

Shops

I like shopping, especially in sports shops. Glasgow city centre has lots of different shops!

There aren't any shops that I can walk to on my own from my house. We go to a shopping centre nearby, but we have to drive to get there.

I like going to the sports shops in Glasgow to look at the football stuff they have, like the new *Rangers* strips.

My parents buy a lot of food from the supermarket, but we buy things from a local *kosher deli* too. The food is really nice!

▲ **Inside the kosher deli.**

Sometimes we have *bagels* with salmon and cream cheese. Yum!

School

I go to a Jewish school called Calderwood Lodge. My teacher is called Miss Jack.

▲ Me with Miss Jack.

We learn all about our religion and are taught *Hebrew*, which is the original Jewish language. My favourite lesson is gym because we get to play sports like netball and rounders.

There is a *synagogue* in the school where we go to pray.

▶ **Sometimes a *Rabbi* comes to talk to us in assembly.**

I love having chips for lunch, but we only get them about once a month. We never eat meat at school. I take a snack for breaktime, like some fruit or a packet of crisps. I usually eat it in the playground with my friends.

My Friends

I have lots of friends at school, but my best friend is called Dillon. Our parents are friends too!

Dillon goes to my school and comes over to play at the weekends.

▶ My best friends at school.

Dillon's birthday is a few weeks before mine so we have joint birthday parties. This year we might go bowling!

◀ Me playing table football with Dillon.

I've known most of my school friends since I was born! We go to each others' houses and play on the PlayStation. I've got some really good games to play on it.

▶ **Me with my friend Gil.**

Sometimes we play card games like Top Trumps where you have to win all the cards off the other players.

Food

I like lots of different food, but my favourite is chicken nuggets dipped in ketchup.

Jews are only allowed to eat certain foods that are kosher. Kosher means fit or proper.

We can't eat things like pork or shellfish. My family eats kosher food.

◄ **Me eating my breakfast.**

On Friday nights we have a special dinner in honour of *Shabbat*. Shabbat is the Jewish holy day, or day of rest. My grandparents come over and I get to stay up late. We eat *challah*, which is a special bread.

◀ This is challah.

During the festival called *Pesach* (or Passover), we eat a special meal with all of our family at the dining room table.

My Hobbies

I love sport, and my favourite hobby of all is football.

▼ My football class at Maccabi.

I play football with my friends and have classes on Sundays too. Me and my dad support the Rangers team. Sometimes he takes me to watch matches at Ibrox Stadium.

I collect football stickers and buy them with my pocket money. Sometimes my grandparents will buy them for me as a present. If I get two the same, I swap them with my friends.

In the evenings I usually play with my Game Boy or watch TV if I'm tired. I like Cartoon Network and a channel called Boomerang.

▶ **Me and Dayna playing with my Game Boy.**

Languages

I speak English most of the time, but I'm also learning Hebrew.

Hebrew is the language people speak in Israel and most Jews know it. I'm learning it at school and am getting quite good. Some words are hard to say but I can have a conversation if I really try. I usually speak English at home and with my friends and family.

◀ **This book is written in Hebrew.**

22

I also know a bit of French and Spanish. We started learning French at school this year, and I know a few Spanish words because I went to Spain on holiday.

▶ **Me learning French at school.**

◀ **I like helping Maya learn to read.**

Clothes

My mum buys most of my clothes. I like going shopping with her to choose things.

I usually wear jeans, jumpers and t-shirts, but I have to wear a uniform to school. I love wearing my Rangers football strip.

▶ **Me in my Rangers strip.**

When I go to the synagogue (Jewish place of worship) I wear a smart shirt and trousers. Boys and men have to wear a *kippah* to cover their head, and married women wear a scarf or hat as a sign of respect to God. My mum and sister wear dresses or skirts and my dad wears a suit.

▲ Me at the synagogue.

◀ Two of my kippahs.

Religion

We worship in a building called a synagogue, and our holy book is called the Torah.

I pray at a synagogue every Saturday with my mum, dad and sister. Men and boys have to sit separately from women and girls.

The Rabbi stands and prays on a platform, called a bimah, and reads from the Torah. Through the year the Torah is read from beginning to end. The Torah is written in Hebrew, on *scrolls* of *parchment*.

When we read it, we always use a special pointer called a *yad*. We never touch it with our fingers, out of respect.

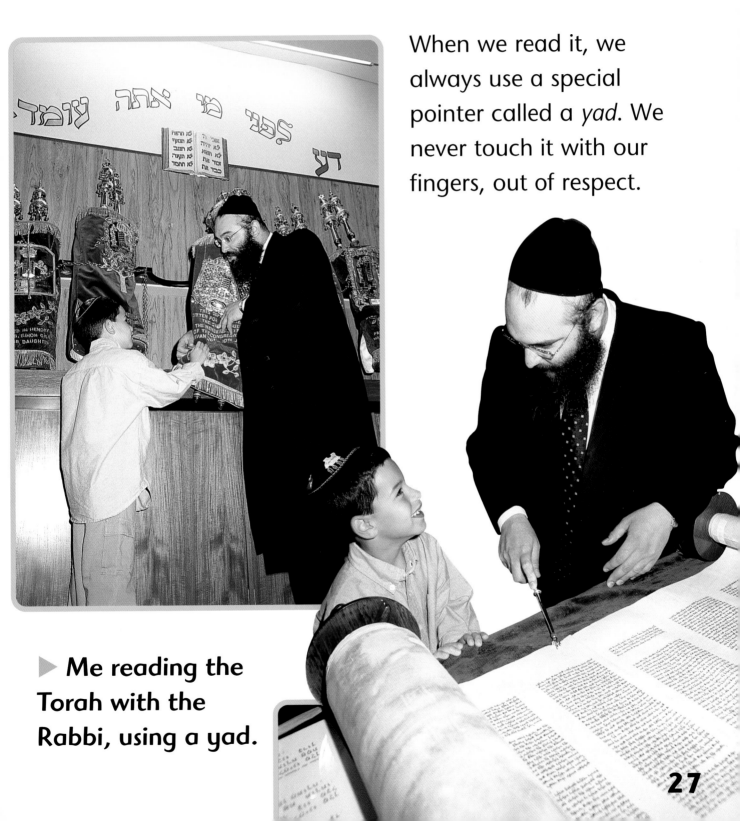

▶ **Me reading the Torah with the Rabbi, using a yad.**

Celebrations

Jews have lots of festivals and celebrations throughout the year, and throughout their lives.

Rosh Hashana is the Jewish New Year festival. We look back at the mistakes we made last year and make *resolutions* for the year ahead.

◀▲ Rosh Hashana cards.

We also eat sweet foods because we are hoping for a sweet year.

◀ I like eating apples dipped in honey at Rosh Hashana.

Hanukah is my favourite festival. It lasts for eight nights in December. We light a different candle every day and get presents too!

▶ **My mum helping me light the candles.**

At the age of 12 or 13, Jewish children are seen as adults. They have a ceremony at the synagogue to celebrate this. It's called bar mitzvah, for boys, and bat mitzvah, for girls.

My cousin Sam is having his bar mitzvah this year and we've bought him a *tallit bag*. It's a traditional bar mitzvah gift.

◀ **A tallit bag.**

29

I like Glasgow

I really like living in Glasgow. I like travelling around and seeing other cities and countries, but I'm glad this is my home.

Glossary

Bagel A type of bread roll that is baked in a ring.

Challah A type of plaited bread that is eaten at Shabbat.

Deli (short for delicatessen) A shop that sells cooked meats, cheeses and ready-made snacks.

Hebrew A language spoken in Israel and by Jewish people.

Jewish Of or related to the religion called Judaism.

Kippah A skullcap worn by male Jews.

Kosher Food that has been prepared in a certain way, according to Jewish law. Kosher literally means fit or proper.

Parchment A thick, high-quality paper. It is traditionally made from the skin of a sheep, goat or calf.

Pesach An eight-day Jewish festival held in Spring, also known as Passover.

Rabbi A Jewish religious leader.

Rangers One of Glasgow's main football teams.

Resolution A promise that you will try to do something.

Scroll A long roll of paper or parchment.

Shabbat This is the Jewish holy day or day of rest. The word 'Shabbat' means Sabbath in Hebrew. Shabbat begins at sunset on Friday evening, and ends at nightfall on Saturday.

Synagogue The Jewish place of worship.

Tallit bag A bag holding a special prayer shawl called a tallit. Jewish men wear the shawl when they pray. A tallit bag is a traditional bar mitzvah gift.

Yad A special pointer that is used to follow the text in the Torah.

Index